A Parents Resource Guide to Cultivate Early Education

" Where You The Parent Can Be Your Childs Most Influential Teacher"

Ages 2 to 6

By: Patricia A.C. Jacobs

Copyright

Published by Patricia A. C. Jacobs
© 2015, Patricia A.C. Jacobs

All rights reserved. No part of this book may be reproduced, stored in or introduced into a retrieval system or transmitted in any means without the expressed written consent of the publisher of this book.

ISBN 978-0-9815658-6-6
ISBN   0-9815658-6-7

First Edition
First Edition Printing, December 2015
1 0 9 8 7 6 5 4 3 2 1

Table of Contents

Introduction……………………………………………1
ABC Chart…………………………………………….2
Uppercase Letter Writing Practice Sheets………..3
Lowercase Letter Writing Practice Sheets………..12
Vowels……………………...………………………...16
Activity Sheet for Writing Vowels……………..17
Consonants…………………………………………18
Activity Sheets for Writing Consonants………..19
Consonant Blend Letters……………………………23
Consonant Blend Activity Sheets.…………….. .24
Tips to Enhance Reading……………….… ……..28
Magical Moments to Learning………………….33
Easy Letter to Word Learning Concepts..……….34
Rhyming Words..……………………………….36
Rhyming Words Activity Sheet……………….…37
Opposite Words..………………………………….40
Opposite Words Activity Shee…………………..41
Name Writing Activity Sheets…………………44
Number Chart 1-100……………………………48
1-20 Number/ Word Recognition in English..…..49
1-20 Number Word Writing in English………….50
1-20 Number / Word Recognition in Spanish..….55
1-20 Number Word Writing in Spanish………….56
1-20 Number to Dot Recognition......……………61

Table of Contents

1-20 Number to Dot Activity Sheets...................63
Color Recognition in English and Spanish...........67
Tips To Easily Learn Colors......................................68
Coloring Activity Sheets..69
Activity Sheets for Drawing Shapes..................80
Days of the Week in English and Spanish...........88
Months in the Year in English and Spanish..........89
Family Name Titles in English and Spanish........90
Childs All About Me Activity Sheets...................91
Parts of the Body in English and Spanish...........96
Five Senses...97
Five Senses Activity Sheets......................................98
Facial Expressions...103
Facial Expressions Activity Sheets...................104
Five Food Groups..109
Five Food Groups Activity Sheets.....................111
Pet Names in English and Spanish....................116
Draw your Favorite Pet Activity sheet..............117
Farm Animal Names in English and Spanish.......118
Draw your Favorite Farm Animal Activity Sheet..119
The Four Seasons...120
Four Seasons Activity Sheets..............................121
Words that Represent Weather Conditions...........125
Weather Activity Sheets..126
Learning Tips to Strengthen Fine Motor Skills.....128
Shoe Tying Chant...129

Introduction

Welcome to "A Parents Guide to Cultivate Early Education "where simple techniques can open up a new world into the beginning stage of learning. This book was designed to be an aid in helping parents to interact one on one with their child in reaching the basic foundations in early learning with levels of growth that will enhance and increase their learning. This book is composed of not only teachable material but workable materials and techniques to help you in fostering your child learning. From years of hands on experience I have found out that learning should be fun and exciting , how something is taught is just as important as what is being put forth to learn .

A B C Chart

Aa Bb Cc Dd Ee Ff

Gg Hh Ii Jj Kk Ll

Mm Nn Oo Pp Qq Rr

Ss Tt Uu Vv Ww Xx

Yy Zz

Uppercase Letter Writing Practice Sheets
(with easy to follow directions)

To write the letter A draw two slanted lines having the tips of both lines coming together at the tip and then draw a line in the middle to connect both slanted lines.

To write the letter B draw one line and two circles.

To write the letter C draw a half circle to the left.

To write the letter D draw a line down and one circle.

To write the letter E draw a line down with three lines going outward.

To write the letter F draw a line down with two lines going outward.

To write the letter G draw a half circle to the left, draw a line going inside the half circle and then draw the line outward. Hint (the child can think of the letter G like a parking garage)

_____

_____

To write the letter H draw two lines going down and draw one line in the middle to connect the two lines. Hint (the H is tall)

_____

_____

To write the letter I draw a line going across and draw a line going across the bottom now draw a line down the middle. Hint (the I is wide)

_____

_____

To write the letter J draw a line down and curve to the left. Hint (it is the shape of an umbrellas handle)

_____

- -

_____

To write the letter K draw a line down , go back to the middle and kick up, go back to the middle and kick down . Hint (the k is kicking)

_____

- -

_____

To write the letter L draw a line down and a little line to the bottom.

_____

- -

_____

To write the letter M draw a line up, down, back up and down again .Hint(hold up your pinky, ring finger and middle finger and turn them downwards)

To write the letter N draw a line up, down and back up again. Hint (it's almost half of the letter M)

To write the letter O draw a circle.

To write the letter P draw a line and draw a small circle to the top.

To write the letter Q draw a circle and put a short line hanging down from the bottom.

To write the letter R draw a line and a small circle to the top now go back to the middle and draw a line downward.

To write the letter S draw the shape of a snake.

To write the letter T draw a line going across now draw a line down the middle.

To write the letter U draw a line down and curve up to the right. Hint (it looks like a long happy face)

To write the letter V draw a slanted line down and a slanted line going up. Hint (hold up the pointer finger and middle finger)

_____

- -

_____

To write the letter W draw a line down , up , down and back up again .Hint (it's an upside down letter M)

_____

- -

_____

To write the letter X draw a slanted line, now draw another slanted line over it. Hint (exit, X marks the spot)

_____

- -

_____

To write the letter Y draw a tiny letter v and draw a line from the middle downward.

To write the letter Z draw lines that go zip, zip and zip. Hint (it thundered the letter Z as in lightning bolts)

Lowercase Letter Writing Practice Sheets

a_____

b_____

c_____

d_____

e_____

f_____

g_____

h_____

i_____

j_____

k_____

l_____

m_____

n_____

o_____

p_____

q_____

r_____

s_____

t_____

u_____

v_____

w_____

x_____

y_____

z_____

Vowels

(a e i o u and sometimes y)

a e i o u

and sometimes

y

Activity Sheet for Writing Vowels

a_____

e_____

i_____

o_____

u_____

y_____

Consonants

b c d f g h

j k l m n p

q r s t v w

x y z

Activity Sheets for Writing Consonants

b_____

c_____

d_____

f_____

g_____

h_____

j_____

k_____

l_____

m_____

n_____

p_____

q_____

r_____

s_____

t_____

v_____

w_____

x_____

y_____

z_____

Consonant Blend Letters

bl   br   ch   cl   cr

dr   fl   fr   gl   gr

kl   kr   pl   pr   ry   sc

sh   sl   sm   sn   sp   st

sw   th   tr   wr

Consonant Blend Activity Sheet

(Words can be made by adding vowels and consonants)

1. _____

2. _____

3. _____

4. _____

5. _____

6. _____

7. _____

8. _____

9. _____

10. _____

11. _____

12. _____

13. _____

14. _____

15. _____

16. _____

17. _____

18._____

19._____

20._____

Tips to Enhance Reading Skills

1. Let your child know that you will be a part of their learning.

2. Establish a study place and a time limit in which you will be spending time in helping your child to learn.

3. It is important to consider the attention span of your child.

4. Being patient and being consistent is the key to seeing results.

5. While the child is recognizing their alphabet letters and the sound of each letter help them also to distinguish which letters are vowels and which ones are consonants.

6. After the child is able to recognize the letter and the sound that the letter makes, begin to introduce to the child a word family along with some sight words.

Starter list of word families

at	**en**	**in**	**ig**	**an**	**im**
pat	pen	win	fig	fan	Tim
rat	hen	fin	wig	ran	him
hat	ten	tin	pig	man	Jim

og	**un**	**am**	**ar**	**op**	**ip**
fog	fun	ham	car	mop	tip
hog	run	jam	far	top	hip
jog	sun	ram	tar	bop	chip

Starter List of Sight Words

we	do	he	me	came	who
in	out	we	then	a	it
big	have	all	off	could	see
you	too	my	like	the	what
out	here	they	with	as	look
on	I	are	got	want	to
at	is	am	of	yes	play
was	go	jump	from	not	us
there	little	saw	so	this	where
went	can	but	by	away	him
eat	day	get	for	here	who
read	run	her	said	that	has
because					

7. Color Sight Words
brown
white
black
green
yellow
red
purple
pink
blue

8. Number Sight Words
one
two
three
four
five
six
seven
eight
nine
ten

9. Help your child to begin making short sentences or phrases with combining word families and sight words together.
Example:
I saw a big cat.
Hop on the ball.
The sun is hot.
I can flip.
Jim went to play.
The hen is red.

10. If you know your letters and the sound that each letter makes then you can begin to read.

11. Remember that letters are put together to make words and words are put together to make sentences and sentences are put together to make paragraphs.

12. Picture books can be used to show the child that pictures in a book represent words and that the picture can be a guide to reading. Example: There may be a picture in the book of a boy hitting a ball .The words underneath the picture may read .The boy is hitting the ball.

13. If the child does not know the word have them to sound out each letter one at a time, and then say the entire word.
Example: **P** **a** **t** , then say the entire word **Pat** .

14. If your child is having a hard time comprehending that in which you are trying to teach them , then incorporate in the teaching a word or an item that your child can identify with.

Magical Moments to Learning

1. Magical moments throughout a child day can promote opportunities to stronger parent / child relationship.

2. As you sit down to begin dialogue with your child it is very important that you establish eye contact.

3. When having a conversation with your child ask questions that will require the child to use their thinking skills.

4. While driving down the road ask your child to tell you about some of the things that they are noticing out of the window.

5. During dinner time ask your child about their day.

6. While your child is dressing have them to name the color of clothing that they are wearing.

7. You can play I spy games and have your child to find an item that is a particular color.

8. Make flash cards and have your child to name that color card.

9. Start a conversation about time spent while at the park, on the way home from a vacation, a trip, time spent at the library, the doctor office, at the beach or about a special outing.

10. Incorporate everyday routines into a day of learning every day.

Easy Letter to Word Learning Concepts

(With the listed words below create a conversation to strengthen language and one on one communication.)

Example: A is for apple
Ask your child where do they think apples come from and how do they grow .While grocery shopping visit the apple section and point out to your child the different types of apples along with the colors and the different types of foods that can be made with apples. You can also have your child to draw an apple tree and count how many apples are on the tree. Expand, explore, be creative and have fun in the world of words.

A is for apple arm ant and animal.
B is for baby bear bubbles and barn.
C is for candy cat car and corn.
D is for door duck daddy and dinner.
E is for egg ear eye and eagle.
F is for farm finger food and face.
G is for girl giggle goat and game.
H is for house hand horse and ham.
I is for ice insect inchworm and ice cream.

J is for jungle jam juice and jelly.
K is for kind king kitchen and kite.
L is for laugh love leg and log.
M is for milk monkey money and mommy.
N is for nose nice nest and nine.
O is for onion octopus one and oval.
P is for puppy pie pickle and paint.
Q is for queen quack quarter and quick.
R is for rain river rat and ring.
S is for snail soft sun and smell.
T is for touch turtle top and table.
U is for up under umbrella and unicorn.
V is for van vegetable violin and volcano.
W is for watch worm water wiggle.
X is for x-ray xylophone box fox.
Y is for yarn yacht yoyo yam.
Z is for zebra zoo zipper zero.

Rhyming Word List

man	can
bat	pat
top	hop
pig	dig
ball	tall
door	floor
rug	tug
tree	see
shoe	glue
sock	rock
sun	fun
box	fox

Activity Sheet for Writing Rhyming Words

1. _____

2. _____

3. _____

4. _____

5. _____

6. _____

7. _____

8. _____

9. _____

10. _____

11. _____

12. _____

13. _____

14. _____

15. _____

16. _____

17. _____

18. _____

19. _____

20. _____

Opposite Word List

hot   cold

wet   dry

hard   soft

up   down

left   right

under   above

night   day

long   short

happy   sad

Activity Sheet for Writing Opposite Words

1._____

2._____

3._____

4._____

5._____

6._____

7._____

8._____

9._____

10._____

11._____

12._____

13._____

14. _____

15. _____

16. _____

17. _____

18. _____

19. _____

20. _____

Name Writing Activity Sheets

Number Chart 1-100

1	2	3	4	5	6	7	8	9	10
11	12	13	14	15	16	17	18	19	20
21	22	23	24	25	26	27	28	29	30
31	32	33	34	35	36	37	38	39	40
41	42	43	44	45	46	47	48	49	50
51	52	53	54	55	56	57	58	59	60
61	62	63	64	65	66	67	68	69	70
71	72	73	74	75	76	77	78	79	80
81	82	83	84	85	86	87	88	89	90
91	92	93	94	95	96	97	98	99	100

1-20 Number / Word Recognition in English

1 one
2 two
3 three
4 four
5 five
6 six
7 seven
8 eight
9 nine
10 ten
11 eleven
12 twelve
13 thirteen
14 fourteen
15 fifteen
16 sixteen
17 seventeen
18 eighteen
19 nineteen
20 twenty

1-20 Number Word Writing in English

_____

one ---------------------------------------

_____

two---------------------------------------

_____

three---------------------------------------

_____

four---------------------------------------

_____

_____

five-------------------------------------

_____

_____

six---------------------------------------

_____

_____

seven-----------------------------------

_____

_____

eight------------------------------------

_____

_____

nine------------------------------------

_____

_____

ten-------------------------------------

_____

_____

eleven----------------------------------

_____

_____

twelve----------------------------------

_____

_____

thirteen-----------------------------------

_____

_____

fourteen-----------------------------------

_____

_____

fifteen------------------------------------

_____

_____

Sixteen------------------------------------

_____

_____

seventeen----------------------------------

_____

_____

eighteen ----------------------------------

_____

_____

nineteen-----------------------------------

_____

_____

twenty-------------------------------------

_____

1-20 Number / Word Recognition in Spanish

1 uno
2 dos
3 tres
4 cuatro
5 cinco
6 seis
7 siete
8 ocho
9 nueve
10 diez
11 once
12 doce
13 trece
14 catorce
15 quince
16 dieciseis
17 diecisiete
18 dieciocho
19 diecineve
20 veinte

1-20 Number Word Writing in Spanish

uno --

dos --

tres --

cuatro --

cinco ---

seis --

siete ---

ocho --

nueve --

diez ---

once ---

doce ---

trece ---

catorce ---

quince --

dieciseis ---

diecisiete --

dieciocho --

diecinueve--

veinte---

1-20 Number to Dot Recognition

1 .
2 . .
3 . . .
4 . . . .
5 . . . . .
6 . . . . . .
7 . . . .
8 . . . .
9 . . . .
10 . . . .
11 . . . .

12 ....
13 ....
14 ....
15 ....
16 ....
17 ....
18 ....
19 ....
20 ....

1-20 Number to Dot Activity sheets
(draw the number of dots on the line to represent the number)

1 _____

2 _____

3 _____

4 _____

5 _____

6 _____

7 _____

8 _____

9 _____

10 _____

11 _____

12_____

13_____

14_____

15_____

16_____

17_____

18_____

19_____

20_____

Color Recognition in English and Spanish

Red   -   rojo

Orange   -   anaranjado

yellow   -   amarillo

green   -   verde

blue   -   azul

purple   -   morado

brown   -   café

black   -   negro

white   -   blanco

pink   -   rosado

grey   -   gris

Tips to Easily Learn Colors

1. Use items that the child can easily identify with.

2. Nature / Environment
    The sky is blue.
    The grass is green.
    The stop sign is red.
    The bus is orange.
    The dog is brown.
    The wheels are black.

3. Fruits / Vegetables
    Apples are red.
    Oranges are orange.
    Bananas are yellow.
    Green beans are green.
    Blue berries are blue.
    Grapes are purple.
    Potatoes are brown.
    Olives are black.

Coloring Activity Sheets

Draw something red.

Draw something orange.

Draw something yellow.

Draw something green.

Draw something blue.

Draw something purple.

Draw something brown.

Draw something black.

<u>Draw something white</u>

Draw something pink.

Draw something grey.

Activity Sheets for Drawing Shapes

Draw a square shape.

Draw a star shape.

Draw a rectangular shape.

Draw a diamond shape.

Draw a circle shape.

Draw a heart shape.

Draw a triangle shape.

Draw an oval shape.

Days of the Week in English –Spanish

Sunday - domingo

Monday - lunes

Tuesday - martes

Wednesday - miercoles

Thursday - jueves

Friday - Viernes

Saturday - sabado

Months in the Year in English – Spanish

January - enero

February - febrero

March - marzo

April - abril

May - mayo

June - junio

July - Julio

August - agosto

September - septiembre

October - octubre

November - oviembre

December - diciembre

Family Name Titles in English and Spanish

man	hombre
woman	mujer
father	padre
mother	madre
baby	be be
son	hijo
daughter	hija
boy	chico
girl	chica
brother	hermano
sister	herman
grandpa	abuelo
grandma	abuela

Childs All About Me Activity Sheets

Draw a picture of yourself.

Draw a picture of your family.

Draw a picture of your best friend.

Draw a picture of your favorite food.

Draw a picture of your favorite toy.

Parts of the Body in English and Spanish

hand - mano

face - cara

head - cabeza

leg - pierna

arm - brazo

foot - pie

hair - pelo

nose - nariz

mouth - boca

eyes - ojos

teeth - dientes

ears - orejas

Five Senses

We use our hands to touch

We taste with our mouth

We smell with our nose

Our ears are used for hearing

We use our eyes for seeing

Five Senses Activity Sheets

Draw a picture of your hands.

Draw a picture of your mouth.

Draw a picture of your nose.

Draw a picture of your ears.

Draw a picture of your eyes.

Facial Expressions

Happy

Sad

Excited

Mad

Crying

Facial Expressions Activity Sheets

Draw a facial expression that represents the word Happy

Draw a facial expression that represents the word
Sad

Draw a facial expression that represents the word Excited

Draw a facial expression that represents the word
Mad

Draw a facial expression that represents the word Crying

Five Food Groups

Protein
Turkey
Chicken
Egg
Fish
Pork
Beef
Peanut butter beans

Grains
Cereal
Rice
Wheat
Pasta
Bread

Fruits
apples
oranges
grapes
banana
strawberries
watermelon
pineapple
raisins
cantaloupe

__Vegetables__
Carrots
Corn
Greens
Peas
Cabbage
Broccoli
Green beans
Sweet potatoes

__Dairy__
Milk
Butter
cheese
Ice cream

Five Food Groups Activity Sheets

Draw a picture of your favorite protein food.

Draw a picture of your favorite grain food.

Draw a picture of your favorite fruit.

Draw a picture of your favorite vegetable.

Draw a picture of your favorite dairy product.

Pet Names in English and Spanish

dog   perro

cat   gato

bird   pajaro

turtle   tortuga

puppy   cachorro

rabbit   conejo

mouse   rato'n

snake   culebra

frog   runa

fish   pez

Draw Your Favorite Pet Activity Sheet

Farm Animal Names in English and Spanish

pig   el cerdo

cow   la vaca

sheep   la oveja

donkey   burro

turkey   pavo

horse   caball

chicken   pollo

goat   cabra

rabbit   conejo

bull   torro

Draw Your Favorite Farm Animal Activity Sheet

The Four Seasons

Spring   flowers bloom

Summer   trips to the beach

Fall   leaves change color

Winter   colder weather

Four Seasons Activity Sheets

Draw a Spring Season picture.

Draw a Summer Season picture.

Draw a Fall Season picture.

Draw a Winter Season picture.

Words that Represent Weather Conditions

rainy

freezing rain

thunderstorm

cloudy

sunny

snowy

windy

hail

tornado

Hurricanes

Weather Activity Sheets

Draw a sunny day picture.

Draw a rainy day picture.

Learning Tips to Strengthen Fine Motor Skills

1. Practice drawing lines from one side of the paper to the other.

2. Draw with a writing tool onto paper in different directions.

3. Practice cutting, folding and tearing paper.

4. Thread beads.

5. Shape play dough into different objects or letters.

6. Pick up objects with a clothes pin and place them into a container.

7. Finger painting.

8. You can draw different sizes of circles onto paper and have your child to slowly color in the circles with a marker or crayon.

Shoe Tying Chant

Stand them up

(Stand up the two strings separately)

Make a knot

One bunny ear

(Gather one string up like a bunny ear and hold)

Two bunny ears

(Gather up the other string like a bunny ear and hold)

Roll it over

(Roll over the first bunny ear around the second bunny ear and pull it through the opening hole and magic.)

A Word of Thanks

I hope that the information provided has and will continue to be a guide for you as you assist your child in meeting their educational needs.

Remember to incorporate everyday routines into a day of learning every day.

Thank You
Patricia A. C. Jacobs

Authors Contact Information
ppatsdesire@aol.com

www.ingramcontent.com/pod-product-compliance
Lightning Source LLC
Chambersburg PA
CBHW041702160426
43202CB00002B/9